Another Beginning Word Book
by Cynthia Basil illustrated by Janet McCaffery

BREAKFAST
IN THE
AFTERNOON

William Morrow and Company   New York 1979

Library of Congress Cataloging in Publication Data

Basil, Cynthia.
    Breakfast in the afternoon.

Summary: An easy-to-read introduction
to the origin and meaning of familiar compound words.
1. English language — Compound words — Juvenile literature.
2. English language — Word formation — Juvenile literature.
[1. English language — Compound words]
I. McCaffery, Janet.   II. Title.
PE1175.B357   428'.1   78-10366
ISBN 0-688-22175-0
ISBN 0-688-32175-5 lib. bdg.

Printed in the United States of America.
First Edition
1   2   3   4   5   6   7   8   9   10

When you sleep, you may dream about food,
but you don't eat it.
Nighttime is usually a time of fast,
a time when you do without food.

When you wake up,
you **break**, or end, the **fast**.
You eat **breakfast**!
If you sleep until **after** twelve **noon**,
you eat breakfast in the **afternoon**!

Like *breakfast* and *afternoon*,
lots of words are made of two words added together.
Can you add other words together?
? + brush = a brush you clean with every day
? + wear = the clothes you put on first
? + doors = where you go almost every day

tooth+brush = toothbrush

After breakfast you brush and clean your teeth
with your toothbrush.

under+wear = underwear

Because you wear it under all your other clothes,
you put on your underwear first.

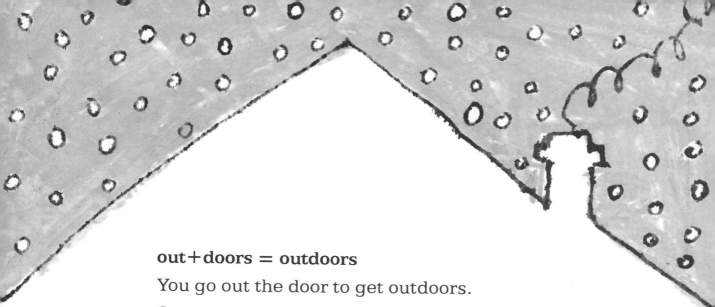

out+doors = outdoors

You go out the door to get outdoors.

Sometimes you go out to play.

play+? = a place outdoors where you play

play+ground = playground

Slides and swings and other things to play on
make a piece of ground into a playground.

Can you add different words to the same word?

sky+? = a very tall building

sky+? = the outline of a city

sky+scraper = skyscraper

Some cities build skyscrapers,
buildings so tall they seem to scrape the sky.

sky+line = skyline

Against the sky all of a city's buildings
seem to be linked in a single line—
the city's skyline.

On the ground all parts of a city
are linked together by a network of streets.
?+walk = part of a street
hop+? = a game you can play there

side + walk = sidewalk
Along the side of a street
is a place to walk —
the sidewalk.

hop + scotch = hopscotch
Scotch is an old word
for a line scratched into something.
When you play hopscotch,
you hop over the line, or scotch,
you scratched on the sidewalk.

You can add animal names
and other words together.
?+neck = a pullover sweater
leap+? = another game

turtle + neck = turtleneck

A turtle's neck folds
when it pulls its head inside its shell.
When you pull on a turtleneck,
its folded neck, or collar,
makes you look a little like a turtle!

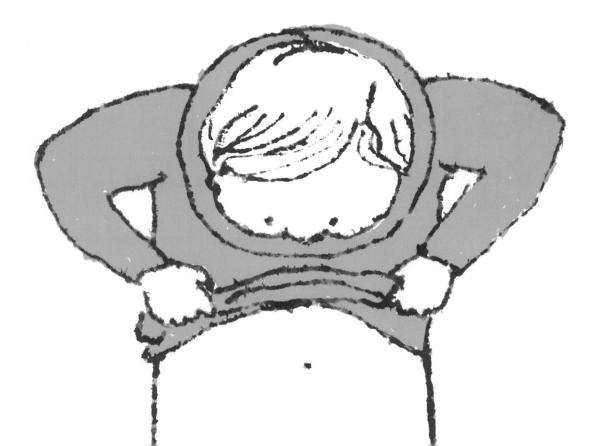

leap + frog = leapfrog
When you play leapfrog,
you leap like a frog over the other players,
who are squatting like frogs!

Can you add words together to make animal names?
butter + ? = a brightly colored insect
wood + ? = a bird that makes holes in trees
cotton + ? = a small rabbit

butter+fly = butterfly

All butterflies fly.

Lots of them are yellow like butter.

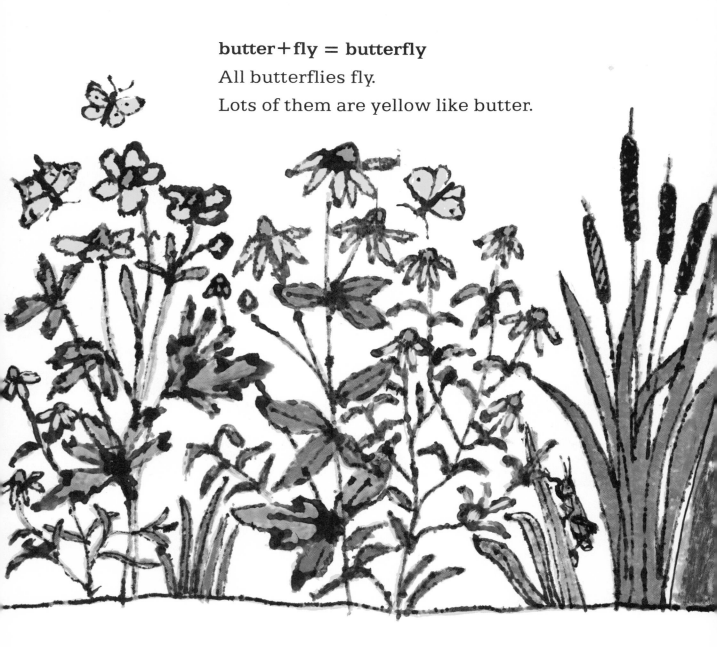

wood + pecker = woodpecker
In the wood of a tree a woodpecker pecks holes
to eat the insects inside and to make a nest.

cotton + tail = cottontail
White, fluffy hairs grow
on the inside of a cotton plant's fruit
and on the underside of a cottontail's tail.

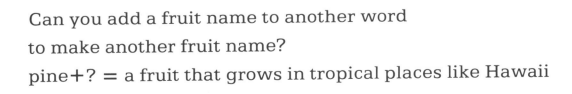

Can you add a fruit name to another word
to make another fruit name?
pine + ? = a fruit that grows in tropical places like Hawaii

pine+apple = pineapple

Pineapple is an old word for a pinecone,
the fruit of a pine tree.
The pineapple we eat got its name
because it looks a little like a big pinecone.

A **grape** is a **fruit** too.
And so is a **grapefruit**!
Grapefruit got its name
because it grows in a bunch like grapes.

You can add many different words to *boat*
to name kinds of boats.
Can you add one word to *boat* in two different ways?

boat + house = boathouse

You can **row**, **sail**, and **speed** over the water in a boat.

When you go ashore, your **rowboat**, **sailboat**, or **speedboat**

may be tied to a dock or kept in a boathouse.

house+boat = houseboat

Most people live in a house on land.
If you live on a boat that looks like a house,
you live in a houseboat!

?+house = not a house, but a way of playing

rough+house = roughhouse

Roughhouse is a rough and rowdy way to play.

If you play that way indoors,

your house may look as if you had turned it upside down.

Sometimes when you turn around,
you can turn yourself upside down.
cart+? = what you do to make that happen

cart + wheel = cartwheel

Stand on your hands, turn around like a cart's wheel,
and land on your feet to do a cartwheel!

With one end of you or the other,
you can make new words.

head + ? = part of a newspaper

? + toe = to walk quietly

? + foot = without shoes and socks

head+line = headline

At the head of a newspaper story
a line of words tells what the story is about.
The big headline at the top of the front page
may be only one word,
but it tells the biggest news.

tip+toe = tiptoe

When you want to move without making a sound,
you walk on the tips of your toes.
You tiptoe!

bare+foot = barefoot

When you take off your shoes and socks,
your feet are bare.
Then you can tiptoe barefoot!

You would be surprised
at how many words are made of two words.
? + day = what each of us has once a year

birth + day = birthday
One day every year
is the date of your birth —
your birthday.

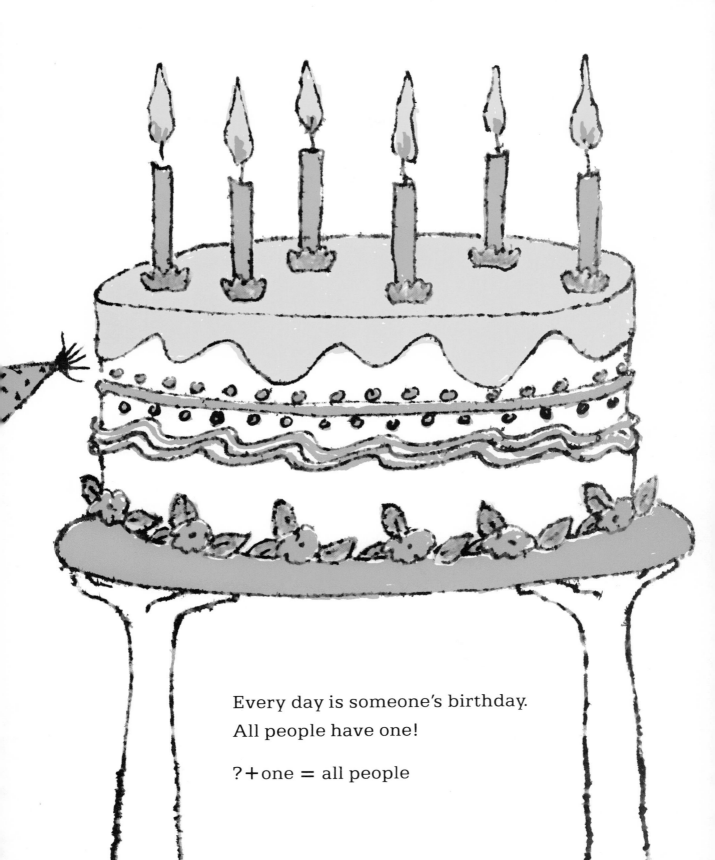

Every day is someone's birthday.
All people have one!

? + one = all people

every + one = everyone

Words made of two words added together
are an everyday part of our language.
Everyone uses some of them every day!

strawberry,
watermelon,
raspberry

butterflies
and a grasshopper

cupcakes for my birthday

skateboard in the playground

pullover
with a turtleneck

upside down and inside out,
outdoors and indoors

sunflower, tablecloth,
clothesline, flowerpots

pancakes for breakfast